British Airways London Eye is conceived and designed by Marks Barfield Architects
British Airways London Eye is an attraction managed by The Tussauds Group

BRITISH AIRWAYS
London eye

Contents

22

18

14

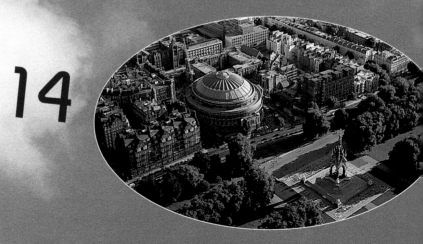

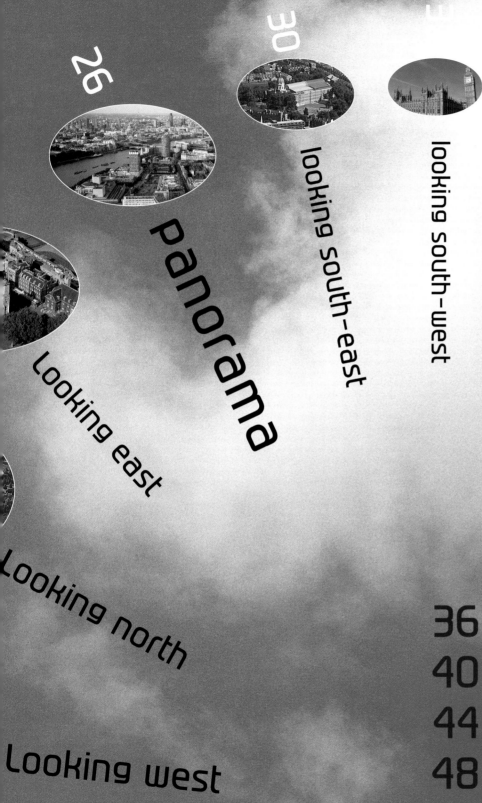

How to use this book

1 The Capsule

First orientate yourself within the capsule. Look for the markings which indicate W N E & S. Match these directionals with the 5 sections of the book. The diagram of the capsule is used throughout this book for orientation.

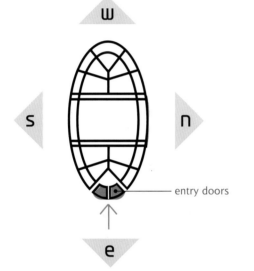

entry doors

3 The Big Panorama

The centre of this book opens out into a spectacular, annotated 360° panoramic view of the city. Use this during the course of your flight – the full panorama will be visible when your capsule reaches its highest point.

4 Looking . . .

2 First Views

Go to First Views (page 12). These are the landmarks that are closest to you, on the banks of the River Thames. You will be able to see these at the beginning of your flight.

Looking West

As the Eye begins to rise, turn to page 14 to view the landmarks Looking West.

Looking West Highlights

Use pages 16-17 to zoom in and view some of the key landmarks in more detail.

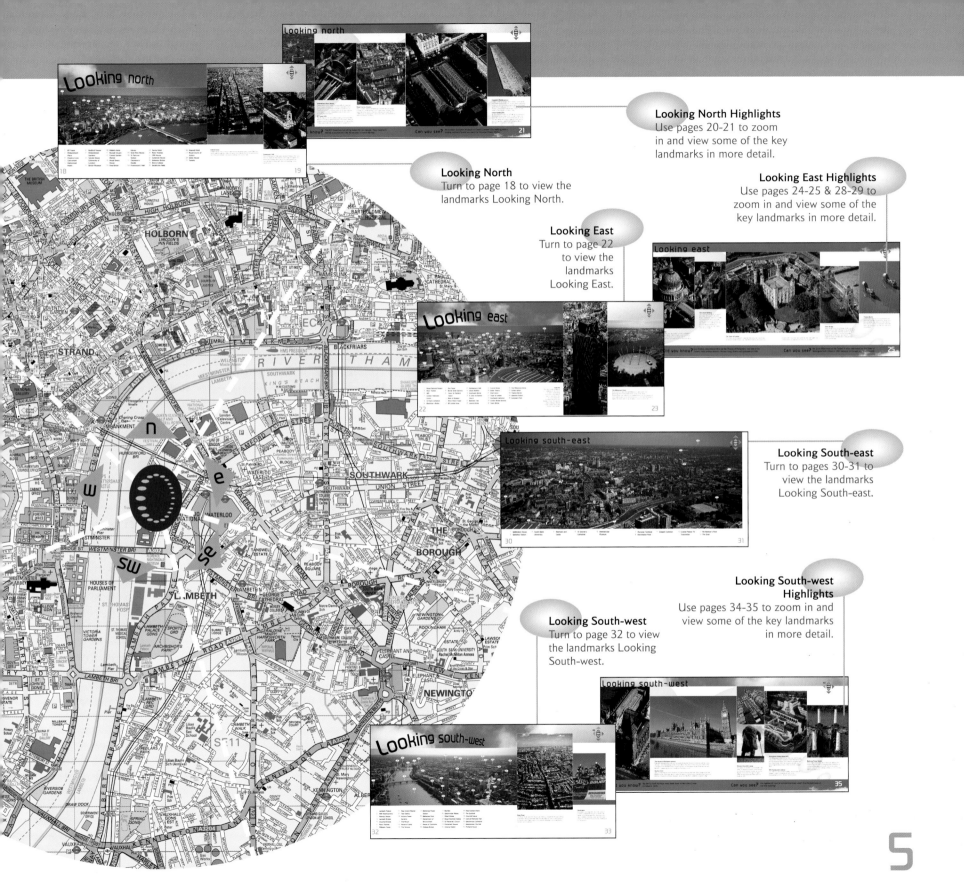

Looking North Highlights
Use pages 20-21 to zoom in and view some of the key landmarks in more detail.

Looking North
Turn to page 18 to view the landmarks Looking North.

Looking East Highlights
Use pages 24-25 & 28-29 to zoom in and view some of the key landmarks in more detail.

Looking East
Turn to page 22 to view the landmarks Looking East.

Looking South-east
Turn to pages 30-31 to view the landmarks Looking South-east.

Looking South-west Highlights
Use pages 34-35 to zoom in and view some of the key landmarks in more detail.

Looking South-west
Turn to page 32 to view the landmarks Looking South-west.

Information

British Airways London Eye is an attraction managed by The Tussauds Group

Opening Times

Summer: 1st April - 10th September 09.00 - 22.00
Winter: 11th September - 31st March 10.00 - 18.00
Opening times are subject to change. Full access and facilities for disabled visitors.

Booking a Flight

We operate a unique timed booking system. You will be able to book a flight time which is either on the hour or half hour. You may arrive for boarding up to 30 minutes before your booked flight time. Please note that your flight is flexible and as long as you arrive at the boarding gate during the half hour before your flight time, then you will be guaranteed your flight. (Please note that boarding takes up to 30 minutes.)

All tickets are subject to availability, non-transferable, non-refundable and not for re-sale, except with the permission of the London Eye Company Ltd.

THERE ARE TWO WAYS TO BOOK A TICKET:

1 CALL **0870 5000 600** (for up to 24 tickets).
This line is for advance bookings only and is an automated service. Please have your credit card details, and the date and time you wish to book ready when you call. Tickets must then be collected from the ticket hall in County Hall at least 15 minutes before you board.
Please note: tickets pre-booked by telephone will not be available for collection until 3 days after the booking is made, and cannot be sent to you by post.

2 Visit the ticket hall within County Hall adjacent to the Eye for both advanced and same day tickets.

Internet

Visit our website at: **www.ba-londoneye.com**

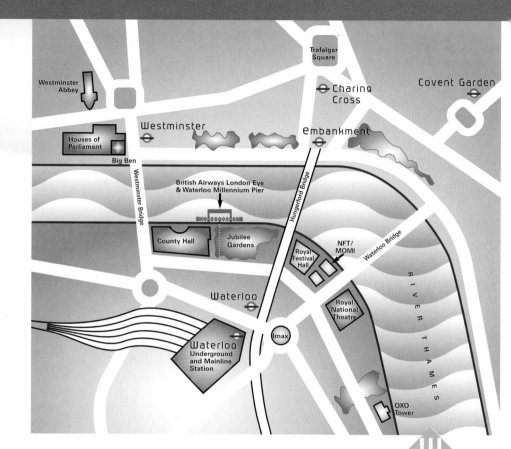

How to Get There

We are located in Jubilee Gardens on the South Bank, between Westminster Bridge and Hungerford Bridge, opposite the Houses of Parliament.
By Tube: Waterloo - 5 minutes, Westminster - 5 minutes, Embankment - 10 minutes.
By Rail: Waterloo International Station - 5 minutes.
By Bus: Numbers 211, 24, 11.
By River: Various river boat operators utilising the new Waterloo Millennium Pier.

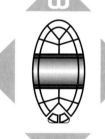

Attraction map

British Airways London Eye

River Thames

Queen's Walk

County Hall

Northern Service Road

Jubilee Gardens

Belvedere Road

(1) County Hall Entrance
(2) Entrance Hall
(3) Information
(4) Ticket Hall
(5) Advanced Ticket Collection
(6) Ticket Hall
(7) Disabled Toilets & Baby Change
(8) Toilets (downstairs)
(9) Costa Coffee
(10) Entrance to Pre-Boarding Area
(11) The Essential Gift Shop
(12) Costa Coffee
(13) Group Waiting Area
(14) Group Leaders/Disabled Ticket Entrance
(15) Coach Drop-Off Point
(16) Waterloo Millennium Pier Entrance
(17) Waterloo Millennium Pier Exit

above A computer generated architectural image of British Airways London Eye.

right above All of the rim sections were built in Holland.

right The 76-feet (23-metre) long hub and spindle about to be lifted by Taklift 1, one of the world's largest floating cranes.

Paris has the Eiffel Tower, New York the Empire State, and now London has British Airways London Eye – an extraordinary icon for an extraordinary city.

As a symbol of regeneration, British Airways London Eye represents the turning of time, celebrating London's past and looking forward to its future. It gives you the opportunity to enjoy one of the world's major cities from a totally new angle. What better way to see all London has

achieved than through the amazing perspectives offered by British Airways London Eye.

In Paris the design of the Eiffel Tower originated in the desire to build something that Parisians and visitors could enjoy, which would become a landmark and which would provide spectacular views. British Airways London Eye is conceived and designed by David Marks and Julia Barfield Architects with the same ideas in mind – a wheel represents the cycle of life, not only creating a

beautiful new landmark but, above all, giving passengers a unique perspective of London.

It has taken seven years to get to the point where you can fly British Airways London Eye. David Marks and Julia Barfield teamed up with British Airways and with The Tussauds Group, and the partners moved together to build this attraction for the new Millennium.

British Airways London Eye was constructed

above Last minute adjustments to one of the bearings inside the hub.

above Passenger capsules under construction in France.

piece by piece throughout Europe. As the biggest observation wheel ever designed, there was no single place where it could be built:

Diameter:	135 metres (450 feet)
Weight :	1,900 tonnes
Weight of a single cable:	1.5 tonnes
Speed:	0.26m/s
Time to revolve:	30 minutes
Viewing distance:	25 miles/40 km

But it is not simply the scale of British Airways London Eye that makes it such a special place from which to view London. Because it is situated on the banks of the River Thames, in the centre of the city, it overlooks many of the city's most famous and impressive landmarks. London grew up around the River Thames because for centuries the river was the main means of travelling through the city and of communicating with other Londoners. As a result, many of the oldest and most important buildings in the city are on its banks and therefore clearly visible from British Airways London Eye.

This is a truly European project. The main structure was built in Holland, using tubular steel provided by British Steel; the hub and spindle were cast in the Czech Republic; the bearings, which allow the rim to turn, were made in Germany; the cables were made in Italy and the capsules were made in France.

An amazing design

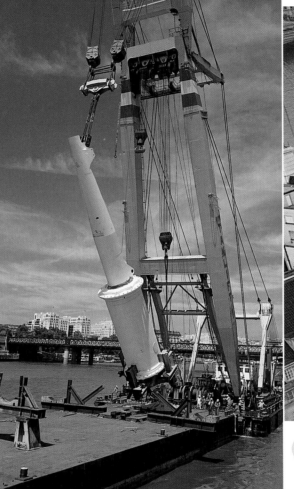

above One of the first sections of the rim to arrive in London, here passing through the Thames Barrier.

below To make sure that the barges could pass under the bridges on the Thames, the height of the river had to be monitored.

left Taklift 1 lifts the hub and spindle off a barge onto a temporary platform.

Once all the components had been made, the site, next to the Thames, allowed British Airways London Eye to be assembled in a unique way. Each piece was sailed up the river by barge – the heaviest part was the hub and spindle, weighing 330 tonnes. British Airways London Eye was then assembled horizontally on temporary platforms built up from the river bed. A detailed survey of the river bed had to be undertaken to decide where the best place would be to position these platforms and to test

the weights that they could bear. Care had to be taken too to ensure that river traffic was not disrupted during construction.

The rim sections were joined together first, lifted into place by Taklift 1, one of Europe's largest floating cranes, which can carry 800 tonnes at a time. The A-frame legs were then attached to the hub and spindle which were connected to the rim by steel cables. The legs were founded deep beneath the ground in Jubilee Gardens, but

are hinged at their base, and so were used to gently lift the rim up from the river into a vertical position. The massive 1,900-tonne structure was lifted into place in stages and then firmly anchored by cables into Jubilee Gardens. Only when British Airways London Eye was in its final position were the passenger capsules attached to its rim.

Remember as you fly over London today that you will be enjoying unparalleled views of the

above British Airways London Eye is almost complete as the final rim section is lifted into place.

city's skyline. When you reach the top you will be at the highest point in London accessible to the public – 450 feet (135 metres). Only Tower 42 (NatWest Tower), Canary Wharf and the BT Tower, which are closed to the public, are taller.

The specially designed capsules in which you will fly were designed by David Marks and Julia Barfield Architects to help you see out from all sides. Because they are attached on the outside of the rim of British Airways London Eye and overhang the river, none of the rim structure obscures the view. The design is unique. On a clear day you will be able to see for 25 miles – as far as Heathrow Airport and Windsor Castle. And if you fly British Airways London Eye at night you will see a very different city. This is illustrated in the 'London by Night' section.

Use this book during your flight in conjunction with the commentary inside the capsules. It will tell you more about the amazing views you are seeing and let you zoom in on some of the most interesting landmarks to view in more detail.

London has some fantastic sights, but don't forget that a city is nothing without the people who live in it. Our 'Green London' and 'People' sections will give you an insight into what it is really like to live in the capital.

Have an extraordinary flight on this, Britain's most extraordinary new attraction.

First views

British Airways London Eye stands on the banks of the River Thames and many of London's most famous landmarks are nearby. This is no coincidence. It is because of the river that London came to be here in the first place.

The Romans settled Londinium at the beginning of the first millennium because the river was vital to trade and travel. The city grew out from here but the river was always at its heart, bringing and exporting goods for sale around the world and providing a safe alternative to travelling by road.

But the river brought problems too. Flooding and freezing were frequent, and pollution was expected in such a busy waterway. The 19th-century innovations of Bazelgette's sewerage system and the creation of the Embankment, which put a buffer between the city and the river, helped a great deal. The Thames Barrier is now London's first defence against floods.

The relationship of the Thames to London changed profoundly when the big container ships of the 20th century could no longer navigate the river and went elsewhere. Since then, the Thames has become a source of pleasure to Londoners. River bank developments have brought restaurants, galleries and entertainment centres, all with magnificent views of the city.

The RAF Monument
This golden eagle sits on the North Bank – in memory of all ranks of the RNAS, RFC, RAF and those Air Forces from every part of the British Empire who fought in the two world wars.

Westminster (left)

Look to your immediate south to see the unmistakable Houses of Parliament and Big Ben, Westminster Bridge, the unusual Portcullis House building (opposite Big Ben), the large white Ministry of Defence building (with the green roofs) and Whitehall Court, which is especially beautiful when lit up at night.

County Hall

Right next door to the Eye, and once home to London's governing body, the Greater London Council, County Hall now houses British Airways London Eye, the Marriott Hotel and London Aquarium.

The North Bank (left)

London's main shopping and entertainment areas (the West End, Soho, Covent Garden), as well as its financial heartland (the City) are to the north. Here you see Hungerford Bridge and Embankment Place, the BT Tower, Cleopatra's Needle, and Waterloo Bridge.

The South Bank

To your immediate east is the South Bank, London's cultural heartland. The South Bank boasts the largest concentration of cultural facilities in the world. Here you can see the Royal Festival Hall, the Hayward Gallery, the BFI National Film Theatre, the Royal National Theatre and the BFI London Imax cinema.

Looking west

28 Central London Mosque

29 Oxford Street

30 Regent's Park

31 St Martin-in-the-fields

32 Leicester Square

South Kensington
Bordering Hyde Park, this is one of the most exclusive places to live in London. This area is often called 'Albertopolis' because the Albert Memorial and the Royal Albert Hall, in the foreground here, were dedicated to her late husband by Queen Victoria. As with many of London's residential areas, it is surprisingly green.

The West End
Forging into Piccadilly Circus like the bow of a ship, is the busy heart of the West End. Shaftesbury Avenue, on the left, is home to some of London's many theatres and Piccadilly Circus has, at its centre, the famous statue of Eros.

Buckingham Palace (above)
Buckingham Palace is the official residence of the British Monarchy (though most British monarchs have lived elsewhere), where the Queen and members of the royal family live and receive important visitors. If the Royal Standard is flying, the Queen is at home.

Trafalgar Square (below)
One of the most famous landmarks in London, Nelson's Column, erected to commemorate Admiral Nelson, who lost his life at the Battle of Trafalgar in 1805, is here. From the air it is the fountain pools that are the most striking. They are lined with blue tiles to make the water look as brightly coloured as possible.

Number 10 Downing Street
Since 1732, Number 10 Downing Street has been the official residence of the Prime Minister. Its famous black door suggests a small house but this view shows you what a very large property it actually is.

Before the statue of Nelson was put in place, the 14 stonemasons who built it had dinner on top of the column in Trafalgar Square.

London Planetarium & Madame Tussaud's (left)
This green dome is the London Planetarium, which takes you on an intergalactic journey through space. Next door is Madame Tussaud's, one of London's top visitor attractions where millions of visitors get close to the rich and famous every year.

Lord's Cricket Ground (above)
Named after Thomas Lord, who moved his Marylebone Cricket Club (MCC) here in 1814, Lord's is one of the country's most historic cricket grounds. Test cricket is played here and you can clearly see the toll that a busy season takes on the wicket!

Royal Albert Hall (left)
Seen from this angle, the Hall, home to the Proms since 1941 and which grew out of the famous Great Exhibition of 1851, is oval and not round as is often thought. Its glass and iron dome has an internal height of 135 feet (40.5 metres) and now has a sound enhancing system within it to cure its notorious echo.

Can you see? the new Lord's commentary box? This ultra-modern box was recently opened to ensure Test match coverage is as well-observed as possible.

Looking north

Oxford Street
Oxford Street, one of Europe's most famous shopping streets, carves huge tyre marks right through the centre of London from Marble Arch at its westernmost tip to the unmistakable Centrepoint building at its eastern end.

Freemasons' Hall
This is Freemasons' Hall, which was built between 1927 and 1933 as a base for the United Grand Lodge of England. It is an unusual building which stands out clearly amidst the concentration of shops and cafés in the bustling Covent Garden area.

Embankment Place (above)

Embankment Place couldn't be more different from the Royal Courts of Justice and is a perfect example of the juxtaposition of traditional and modern architecture so characteristic of 21st-century London. It sits over Charing Cross station and this extraordinary view shows trains emerging from beneath it.

BT Tower (left)

The BT Tower is the third tallest building in Britain at 584 feet (177.5 metres) high. It was built as the nerve centre of London's telecommunications network and you can see the 57 microwave radio aerials that it uses for transmissions.

Royal Courts of Justice

This crowded complex of buildings that looks like an Oxford College or a medieval town is the Royal Courts of Justice. The large hall in the centre is the main entrance and leads off to 1,000 rooms (including 60 court rooms) which are linked by 3½ miles (5.6 km) of corridors.

Did you know? The BT Tower has two of the fastest lifts in Europe. They travel at 6 metres a second and take 30 seconds to reach the top.

Cleopatra's Needle (above)
Cleopatra's Needle is older than London. Carved out of pink granite in about 1475 BC, it once stood in Heliopolis in Egypt. In 1819 it was presented to Britain and shipped up the River Thames, just like the components of British Airways London Eye! Originally one of a pair, its twin can be found in New York.

Covent Garden (left)
In 1631 Francis Russell, Earl of Bedford, commissioned the famous architect Inigo Jones to build a Piazza here which, since family funds were running low, was to be 'not much better than a barn'. You can clearly see the barn structure here, now home to an extraordinary diversity of covered shops and cafés.

Can you see? the London Transport Museum in Covent Garden? This building with a striking red brick façade was once the Victorian Flower Market.

21

Looking east

30

Tower 42
The most easily identifiable landmark in the City of London, and looking from above rather like an electric razor, this is the 52-storey Tower 42. Commonly known as the NatWest Tower, this was the tallest building in Britain before Canada Tower was built in Canary Wharf.

The Millennium Dome
Built as a focus for national Millennium celebrations, the glistening white Millennium Dome is one of the most extraordinary new additions to London's landscape. Its translucent roof, held in place by twelve yellow masts, is 165 feet (50 metres) high at its centre and strong enough to support a jumbo jet.

The Lloyds Building
This unusual building was designed for Lloyds of London by Richard Rogers Partnership and built in 1986. Its originality lies in its 'inside out' design (the services are located on the outside of the building, with the lifts running up and down the exterior). It reveals its true beauty when lit up at night.

St Paul's Cathedral
From this perspective you can see that St Paul's Cathedral is built in a traditional shape – that of a latin cross. Located in the heart of the City, St Paul's is a constant reminder of the capital's past amidst the innovative modern architecture of its financial hub.

The Tower of London
The Tower has dominated London for 900 years, but is itself now dominated by the modern City. The White Tower in the centre is a

Did you know? Guy Fawkes, who tried to blow up the Houses of Parliament, was one of the Tower's most famous inmates. He was hung, drawn and quartered in 1606.

Key to panorama

1. St Thomas's Hospital
2. Lambeth Palace
3. Lambeth Bridge
4. Vauxhall Bridge
5. Millbank Tower
6. Houses of Parliament
7. Battersea Power Station
8. Windsor Castle
9. Heathrow Airport
10. Big Ben
11. Westminster Abbey
12. Westminster Cathedral
13. Foreign Office
14. St James's Park
15. HM Treasury
16. Buckingham Palace

27. Waterloo Bridge
28. Somerset House
29. Royal Courts of Justice
30. Temple
31. Royal National Theatre
32. St Paul's Cathedral
33. Blackfriar's Bridge
34. Oxo Tower
35. Tower 42 (NatWest Tower)
36. BFI London Imax
37. St John the Baptist Church
38. London Bridge

Southwark

Greenwich

17 18 19 20 21 22

W

41 39 40 42

Mayfair West End

se

26

23

24

Lambeth

2

47

Soho/Chinatown

48

50

51

53

55

Covent Gar

45

44

43

49

52

46

54

fortress which was later surrounded by two outer walls. The Crown Jewels are kept here because it is so secure.

Tower Bridge
Tower Bridge is the most famous of all London's bridges and was built following rioting in the steets by angry citizens who were fed up with having to cross the river by boat. It is a bascule bridge, which means its two sides open and lift. It was originally designed in this way so that tall ships could pass through.

Thames Barrier
London has a history of severe flooding and what look here like delicate silver shoes, are in fact part of the vital defences of the Thames flood Barrier. Each holds hydraulic machinery which can swing gates up from the river bed to stop a flood.

Can you see? the grass-filled moat at the Tower? It once held water but the Duke of Wellington had it filled in 1843 because he thought it a health hazard.

Canary Wharf (left)
This was once a dockyard and Canary Wharf took its name from a Warehouse where Canary Island tomatoes were stored. Now it has been redeveloped and its most famous feature is the spectacular 800-feet (244-metre) high Canada Tower, soaring into the sky like a huge shimmering needle.

The Cutty Sark (left)
This is the magnificent prow of the Cutty Sark, a tea clipper that used to sail the trading routes across the Atlantic and Pacific oceans and is now in dry dock in Greenwich. She won the annual race from London to China in 1871 – taking 107 days!

The Imperial War Museum (above)
This unusual view is of one of the tank guns in front of the Imperial War Museum. The museum was founded in 1917 to tell the story of the First World War and has recorded every battle and war since that day.

Did you know? The Imperial War Museum was once Bethlehem Hospital for the insane. Its name was abbreviated to Bedlam, or 'a confused riot' in modern English.

8

7

5

4

Battersea

2

3

6

1

St. Thomas' Hospital

nden

Bloomsbury

29

30

28

27

31

9

Chelsea

Kensington

12

Victoria

16

11

Westminster

10

14

13

15

e

35

32

East End

18

19

20

21

The City

17

38

Docklands

33 34

Southwark

37

36

22

The Globe Theatre
Looking over the reconstructed Globe it is obvious why Shakespeare called the original Globe, 'this wooden O' in Henry V. The new Globe was opened in 1997.

Waterloo Station (above)
From this angle Waterloo looks like a huge blue caterpillar. Originally planned just to service London, Waterloo is now a major international thoroughfare. It is the capital's main rail link to the rest of Europe, with its frequent Eurostar service to France and Belgium.

Can you see? at Waterloo Station the blue and yellow Eurostar trains heading for Europe?

29

Looking south-east

1 Wellington House
2 Waterloo Station
3 South Bank University
4 Elephant and Castle
5 Christ Church and Upton Chapel
6 Imperial War Museum

se

7   Eurostar Terminal
8   Kennington Park

9   Dulwich Common

10 Crystal Palace TV
    Transmitter

11 Archbishop's Park
12 The Oval

Looking south-west

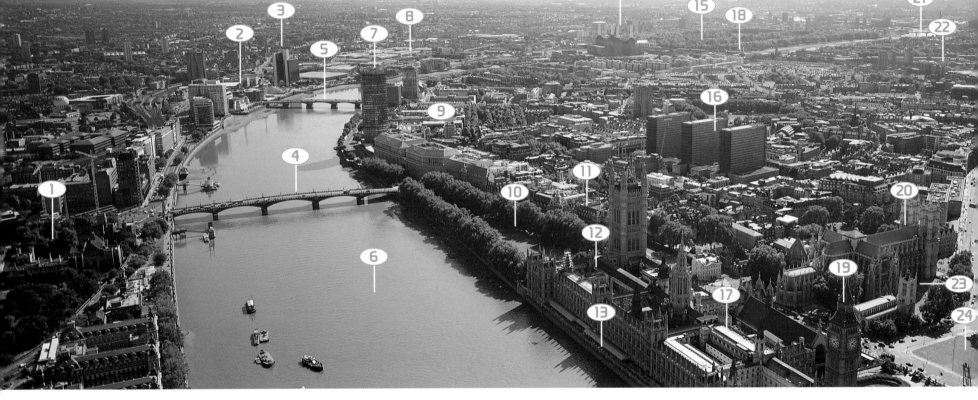

1	Lambeth Palace	8	New Covent Market	14	Battersea Power Station	19	Big Ben
2	MI6 Headquarters	9	Tate Britain	15	Battersea Park	20	Westminster Abbey
3	Alembic House	10	Victoria Tower Gardens	16	Department of Environment	21	Albert Bridge
4	Lambeth Bridge	11	The Atrium	17	House of Commons	22	Royal Hospital Chelsea
5	Vauxhall Bridge	12	House of Lords	18	Chelsea Bridge	23	St Margaret's Church
6	River Thames	13	The Terrace			24	Parliament Square
7	Millbank Tower					25	Victoria Station

26	New Scotland Yard
27	The Guildhall
28	Churchill Statue
29	Central Methodist Hall
30	Westminster Cathedral
31	Westminster City Hall
32	Portland House

King's Road

The King's Road, seen from the air, cuts almost a straight line through Chelsea. Originally it was a private road used only by kings but now it is famous for its boutiques. In the 1960s it was at the heart of 'swinging London' and the first miniskirts were seen here.

Kennington

Kennington was originally, like many parts of London, a village that became a suburb. The laying out of Kennington Park threatened the local tradition of playing cricket and the Oval, which you can see in the centre, was established to compensate.

Looking south-west

The Houses of Parliament (above)
From this unusual perspective you can easily identify the House of Commons and the House of Lords – from the awnings on the terrace. Red is the colour of the Lords and Green of the Commons. From British Airways London Eye you can look down on the Prime Minister and his MPs – something you don't usually get the chance to do!

Big Ben (left)
This is a view that you don't often see of London's famous landmark. Many people think that Big Ben is the clock tower, but it is in fact the name of the bell inside the tower that chimes on the hour. Viewed from British Airways London Eye, Big Ben is suddenly not quite so big!

Did you know? Big Ben's clock has kept exact time more or less since it was installed in 1859.

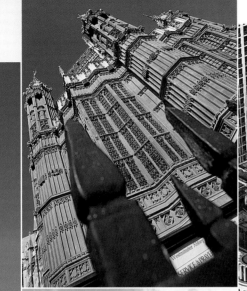

Winston Churchill's statue
The figure of Churchill is unmistakable. His statue in Parliament Square looks towards the Houses of Parliament (you can see the Big Ben clock tower through his legs!). Churchill was laid in state there after his death in 1965.

Westminster Abbey (above left)
The Abbey was consecrated in 1065 and built because Edward the Confessor wanted to make Westminster the base of his government. The country is still governed from Westminster. With the exception of only two, every English monarch since 1066 has been crowned here.

MI6 Headquarters (above)
This elaborate and unusual building, which looks as though it might be made from Lego, is the headquarters of M16 – Britain's secret service.

Battersea Power Station
These highly distinctive white towers are 300 feet (90 metres) high and used to emit pure white smoke due to smoke-washing apparatus inside. The former power station is now a listed building and host to rock concerts, plays and exhibitions.

Can you see? the regimental rows of symmetrical trees which line the balconies of the MI6 building?

Green london

Did you know? London has always had large areas of open space, with five large parks in its central area alone. Despite its growth, it is still a very green city.

Kensington Gardens

Kensington Gardens began, as did many London parks, as private royal land – part of the Kensington Palace estate. It was opened to the public in 1843. The gardens are quiet and unspoilt and you can see here the Round Pound which is a popular feature.

Kensington Palace

The Palace sits within Kensington Gardens and although a part of it is still occupied by members of the royal family, part is open to the public. Kensington Palace will long be associated with Diana Princess of Wales, who lived here.

Hyde Park

Hyde Park was also originally a royal park, and has long been a fashionable place to be seen. A traditional hunting ground, Hyde Park is now home to The Stables, London's oldest original riding centre. It is a popular place to walk and enjoy views of the beautiful Serpentine lake.

Marble Arch

Originally built to stand in front of Buckingham Palace, Marble Arch was moved to its present position at the north-east corner of Hyde Park in 1851. Only senior members of the royal family and the Royal Horse Artillery are allowed to pass through it.

Can you see? the Kensington Palace gates? The sea of flowers placed here in tribute to Diana Princess of Wales is an enduring symbol of the 20th century.

Green london

Regent's Park (left)
Regent's Park is yet another public park created from royal land. It is surrounded by elegant Regency houses such as those you see here. Regent's Park is home not only to an open air theatre but also to London Zoo.

London Central Mosque (above)
At the edge of Regent's Park is the London Central Mosque. It was built in 1978 to provide a place of worship for the rapidly growing Muslim community in London. The main hall is under the golden dome and can accommodate 1,800 worshippers.

The Mall
The Mall runs along St James's Park, from Trafalgar Square to Buckingham Palace. This tree-lined, broad street was originally laid out as a promenade – for much of the 18th century the fashionable citizens of London came here to walk and be seen.

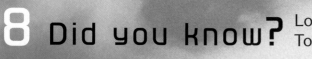

38 **Did you know?** London Zoo's origins lie in the collection of beasts kept by royalty at the Tower of London. The collection moved to Regent's Park in 1834.

Clapham Common (left)
Some of London's green spaces have their origins in the common land that was originally set aside for citizens to feed their animals on. Clapham Common is now a popular spot for a game of football, volleyball, a jog, or simply a stroll.

Battersea Park
Battersea Park was one of the purpose-built parks in London, and opened in 1853. It is popular with cyclists, has an athletics track and boats can be hired to sail on the lake.

Clapham Common
Many green spaces were threatened by the need to build housing in the 19th century as the population of London expanded. But areas like Clapham Common were protected and survive now as tranquil havens in the middle of busy residential areas.

Can you see? the man-made boating lake in Battersea Park? This was opened in 1860 and has a beautiful setting of rocks, gardens and waterfalls.

flight london

| 6 | Canary Wharf | 7 | Oxo Tower | 8 | King's Reach Tower | 9 | London Television Centre | 10 | Royal National Theatre |

Can you see? the Oxo Tower's windows?
They spell out the name of the Tower.

Chinatown (left)
This is one of the elaborate entry gates to Chinatown in Gerrard Street. London's Chinese population numbers 59,000 and during the celebrations for Chinese New Year the area is a riot of colour, as huge crowds from all over London come to follow the Chinese dragon as it snakes its way through the narrow streets.

Piccadilly Circus
Piccadilly Circus has one of the highest concentrations of neon advertising signs in London. It is the gateway to one of the most popular areas for entertainment in the city, and remains an enduring symbol for visitors.

The Houses of Parliament
This magnificent view of the Houses of Parliament shows the building to great effect. If the lights inside are burning, this is because members of the House of Commons and House of Lords often have to work or listen to debates late into the night.

St Paul's Cathedral
Most of London's great landmarks are floodlit, making it easy to pick them out at night. Here, St Paul's Cathedral demonstrates how flood-lighting can enhance the detail of London's impressive architecture.

Can you see? the lights from the Terrace of the Houses of Parliament? The private bars, where members of the Lords and Commons entertain, are here.

43

People

London's population is just over 7 million and in 1998, around 30 million visitors came to the city.

Covent Garden Market
Covent Garden's historic fruit and flower market has been replaced by shops and cafés and is now a bustling shopping and entertainment area. It has become famous as a venue for street entertainers around which crowds gather.

Covent Garden
Street entertainers of every kind come to Covent Garden to perform. You are likely to see comedians, musicians, acrobats and mime artists such as this, in the market and the surrounding Piazza. In the summer a street entertainers' festival is held here.

Paul Smith Shop
London's reputation for fashion was made in the 1960s and 70s when the creations of designers like Mary Quant were first seen on its streets. British designers, such as Paul Smith, whose shop in Covent Garden is shown here, represent all that is contemporary and innovative about the capital.

Did you know? In 1662 Samuel Pepys saw a Punch and Judy show in Covent Garden. A Punch and Judy Festival is held here every year.

People

City Bustle (left above & below)
The City was the first area of London to be settled. Now it is the financial centre of the capital and nearly three quarters of its population work here but live elsewhere. They commute daily by underground, train or bus.

Embankment Gardens
London's green spaces offer its workforce an opportunity for fresh air and relaxation. Here, workers from the Law Courts and other shops and offices nearby enjoy the sun in Embankment Gardens during their lunch break.

Did you know? The City of London has a higher concentration of banks than anywhere else in the world.

Columbia Road Market

The Columbia Road Market is held on Sunday mornings in Shoreditch, in the heart of London's East End. Traditionally home to the 'true Cockney', the market now draws people from all over the city, who come to enjoy the fresh cut flowers, shrubs, and grasses.

Portobello Road Market (above right)

Portobello Road stretches down from Westbourne Grove to Notting Hill. It is one of the most multicultural and fashionable areas of London. At the main market on Saturday, you can buy anything from antiques to curious bric-a-brac items and browse in the designer shops surrounding the market.

Brick Lane (right)

Brick Lane is the centre of London's Bangladeshi community, which numbers in total 106,000 people. The area originated with the sailors who came to London in the 19th century. As well as being a residential area, Brick Lane has many shops selling silks, spices and fabrics, and of course a wealth of authentic Indian restaurants.

DID YOU KNOW? Many of London's markets have long histories. Portobello, for example, was started in the 1870s.

Quiz

Eagle eye quiz

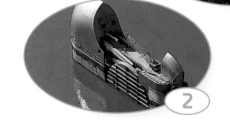

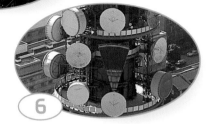

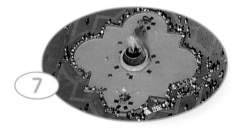

1 Which famous domed concert hall is this? Who was it named after?

2 This is not a ship. What is it?

3 This clock takes its name from the largest bell in the belfry. What is it called?

4 It's not a boat; it's one of the West End's most visited places.

5 Which ancient historic building is this?

6 Where can you find all these satellite dishes?

7 You can't swim in this pool. Where is it?

Super eagle eye quiz

1 Where can you spot these strange golden spikes?

2 This isn't the top of a razor. Which building is it?

3 Reach for the sky inside this huge green dome.

4 This is one of the City's most unusual landmarks.

5 Look east. You can't miss it.

6 This is not a Lego model. What is it?

7 Look north, and this is one of the first buildings you'll see. What is it called?

You will find all the answers on page 52

are proud to bring you the British Airways London Eye. Weeeeeeeeeeeeeeeeeeeeeeeeeeeeeeeeeeeeeeeeeeeeeeeeeeeeeeeeeeeeeeeeeeeeeeeeeeeeeeeeeeeeeeeeeeeeeeeee

BRITISH AIRWAYS
The world's favourite airline

turning a dream into reality

Photo: Marcus Robinson

marks barfield architects
creators of the british airways london eye

50 Bromells Road London SW4 OBG Telephone 0207 501 0180 Fax 0207 498 7103 Email info@marksbarfield.com www.marksbarfield.com

The Tussauds Group is one of the largest operators and developers of visitor attractions with over 10 million guests a year and attractions in the UK, US and Europe. As well as managing and operating British Airways London Eye, The Tussauds Group also brings you:

London Attractions:

Madame Tussaud's

- Where you can mingle with movie stars, be counted amongst world leaders, or line up alongside your favourite sporting heroes. Getting close to the stars has never been easier or more fun at Madame Tussaud's. Close enough to rub shoulders with Naomi Campbell, feel Arnie's muscles and cuddle up to Brad Pitt, there's no knowing who you'll have a close encounter with!

Madame Tussaud's Rock Circus

- Use your backstage pass to go behind the scenes. Take a look at our collection of extraordinary music memorabilia. Experience a multi-media spectacular with Jools Holland. Pay some respect to rock legends like Kurt Cobain and Michael Hutchence in the cemetery. Join Jamiroquai's front man, Jay Kay, Cher and the Spice Girls....all the stars, at an exclusive after-show party.

London Planetarium

- London Planetarium is an amazing sensory experience that appeals to enquiring minds of all ages. After checking in to the Planet Zone, would be astronauts move onto the Space Zone for take-off on an intergalactic journey. Visitors then take off on a Planetary Quest, where the Digistar II and the quest to find a new planet for human habitation is awaiting you.

www.madame-tussauds.com

Other UK and Worldwide Attractions:

Other Madame Tussaud's attractions include Amsterdam, Las Vegas, New York and the Touring exhibition.

www.alton-towers.co.uk

www.warwick-castle.co.uk

www.chessington.co.uk

www.thorpepark.co.uk

Details

First published in 2000 by HarperCollins*Illustrated*
an imprint of HarperCollins*Publishers*
77-85 Fulham Palace Road
London W6 8JB

Reprinted 2000

The HarperCollins website address is:
www.**fire**and**water**.com

A CIP catalogue record for this book is available
from the British Library

ISBN: 0 5833 4674 X

**Design and artworks:
Tanya Devonshire-Jones**

**Mapping for pages 6–7 and cover:
© Bartholomew Mapping Services**

04 03 02 01 00
9 8 7 6 5 4 3 2 1

Colour reproduction by Digital Imaging
Printed and bound in the UK
by Edinburgh Press

Answers to quiz

Eagle Eye Quiz

1 Royal Albert Hall
2 Thames Barrier
3 Big Ben
4 Piccadilly Circus
5 Tower of London
6 BT Tower
7 Trafalgar Square

Super Eagle Eye Quiz

1 The Millennium Dome
2 Tower 42 (NatWest Tower)
3 The London Planetarium
4 Lloyds Building
5 Canada Tower (Canary Wharf)
6 MI6 Building
7 Embankment Place

Did you get them all?